I WANT TO BE A
POLICE OFFICER

By Joanna Brundle

BookLife
PUBLISHING

©2020
BookLife Publishing Ltd.
King's Lynn
Norfolk PE30 4LS

All rights reserved.
Printed in Malaysia.

A catalogue record for this book is available from the British Library.

ISBN: 978-1-78637-961-0

Written by:
Joanna Brundle

Edited by:
William Anthony

Designed by:
Dan Scase

All facts, statistics, web addresses and URLs in this book were verified as valid and accurate at time of writing. No responsibility for any changes to external websites or references can be accepted by either the author or publisher

PHOTO CREDITS:

Images are courtesy of Shutterstock.com.
With thanks to Getty Images, Thinkstock Photo and iStockphoto.

Front Cover - Paul Wishart, happiness time, ChiccoDodiFC, Drop of Light, Alexey Blogoodf, Besjunior
4 – arigato, Drop of Light. 5 – Dave Smith 1965. 6 – Clive Watkins, Lara Ra. 7 – Dave Smith 1965. 8 – Drop of Light, Rat007. 9 – Dave Smith 1965. 10 – Thomas Dutour. 11 – Thomas Dutour. 12 – VGstockstudio. 13 – Marbury. 14 – 1000 Words. 15 – Ms Jane Campbell. 16&17 – eronica Louro, John Roman Images, John Gomez, Peter Titmuss. 18 – Platslee. 19 – Paul Wishart. 20 – Darlene Munro. 21 – Zakrevsky Andrey, miniaria. 22 – KanKhem, yusufdemirci, Naddya. Vector tape: VikiVector

CONTENTS

Words that look like <u>this</u> can be found in the glossary on page 24.

HELLO, I'M PRADHI!

Hello, I'm Pradhi! When I grow up, I want to be a police officer. You could be one too! Let's find out what this job will be like.

4

I want to be a police officer so that I can be an important part of the community. I will help to keep my community safe and peaceful for everyone.

Anybody can be a police officer if they work hard.

WHAT WILL I DO?

These police officers are keeping a large crowd safe.

I will help to keep people and property safe.

I will try to stop people from breaking the law.

I will **arrest** people who have broken the law. These people are called criminals.

I will talk to people who have broken the law or seen a **crime** to find out what happened.

These police officers are helping people who are lost.

HOW WILL I HELP PEOPLE?

Can you think of why someone might call the police?

If there is an **emergency**, people can call the police by calling 999 or 112. I might be one of the police officers who goes to help these people.

I could become a police officer who makes sure that people drive safely and at the right speed. These officers also direct traffic and go to traffic <u>collisions</u>.

WHERE WILL I WORK?

I might work in large crowds of people, such as at sporting events or parades. Police officers make sure that people can move around safely and are not breaking the law.

This police officer is making sure a crowd is safe by the road.

These police officers are <u>patrolling</u> their community on foot.

I might walk or drive around the streets in my community. I will also do some of my work at a police station.

WHAT IS IN A POLICE STATION?

Inside, there is a desk where people can go to speak to a police officer. There are rooms where people who have broken the law or seen a crime are asked questions.

People who have broken the law may need to be kept at the police station. They are kept in <u>cells</u>. Outside the station, there are parking spaces for police cars.

www.cheshire.police.uk

POLICE

All those police cars look the same!

WHAT WILL I WEAR?

I wear a school uniform. Do you? I will wear a uniform when I am a police officer too. I might wear trousers, a shirt, a tie, and a hat.

Shirt

Hat

Tie

Not all police officers wear this uniform.

Trousers

Uniforms help people to see who is a police officer. A bright yellow jacket like this will help me to be seen easily in the dark or in bad weather.

WHAT EQUIPMENT WILL I USE?

Let's have a look at some of the equipment I might use.

Handcuffs – used to hold someone who has been arrested

Radio – used to talk to other police officers

Camera – worn on a vest to record what happens

METROPOLITAN POLICE

VIDEO & AUDIO

HOW WILL I TRAVEL AROUND?

I might drive a police car or van, or I might ride a motorcycle. Some police officers use boats, horses, bicycles or helicopters to travel around.

Police use helicopters to follow criminals and to spot traffic jams and collisions.

Siren

Let's look at a police car.

The lights and siren will warn people that I'm coming.

These coloured patterns mean my car will be seen clearly.

Flashing blue lights

Some officers carry a cuddly toy in their car to comfort children.

POLICE

ORGANISATION 100

19

WHERE COULD I WORK AROUND THE WORLD?

Mounties

The police force in Canada is called the Royal Canadian Mounted Police, or Mounties. Some officers wear a bright red uniform and ride a black horse.

I would love to be a traffic police officer in Italy. They sometimes use very fast supercars to catch drivers who are speeding.

Some police officers in the US work to protect sea turtles and whales.

CAN YOU HELP ME CATCH A THIEF?

One of these people has stolen the chocolate cake. They are all called <u>suspects</u>. Use your finger to trace the path that leads one of the suspects to the cake.

Police officers sometimes use **fingerprints** to catch a thief. Everyone's fingerprints are different. If the suspect's fingerprints are on the cake, they probably stole it.

My fingerprints look like this. What are yours like?

GLOSSARY

ARREST	catch a suspect and take them to a police station
CELLS	small, locked rooms in police stations or prisons
COLLISIONS	crashes involving two or more objects
COMMUNITY	a group of people who live and work in the same place
CRIME	an action or set of actions that are against the law
EMERGENCY	a dangerous situation that requires action
FINGERPRINTS	marks made by a person's fingertips
LAW	a rule or set of rules that people must follow
PATROLLING	keeping watch over an area by walking or travelling around it
PROPERTY	things that belong to people
SUSPECTS	people who are thought to have carried out a crime

INDEX